First Baby Poems

Anne Waldman

Collages by George Schneeman

BlazeVOX [books]

Buffalo, New York

First Baby Poems by Anne Waldman

Copyright © 2009

Published by BlazeVOX [books]

Printed in the United States of America

Book design by Geoffrey Gatza

Cover image and collages by George Schneeman

First published in 1982 by Rocky Ledge Cottage Editions
A second expanded edition appeared in 1983 by Hyacinth Girls Editions.
© 1982, 1983, 2009 Anne Waldman

Thanks to Erik Anderson, Richard Froude, and Reed Bye.

ISBN: 1-934289-91-4   ISBN 13: 978-1-934289-91-4
Library of Congress Control Number: 2008932199

BlazeVOX [books]
14 Tremaine Ave
Kenmore, NY 14217

Editor@blazevox.org

publisher of weird little books

BlazeVOX [books]

blazevox.org

2   4   6   8   0   9   7   5   3   1

B   X

for the grandmothers
Frances LeFevre Waldman
& Dorothy Bye Parmalee

Contents

First Baby Poems

"I feel the Sweet trouble beneath my girdle…"

this live belly—whose?—mine?
dark night, sitting—mind still—whose?
solitude—this mind—mine?
baby—what mind?
minding the breath
minding the mind inside the belly
the belly inside my mind

Seminary Sestina

We live under the eye of the Plain of Six Glaciers
300 people in a rambling chateau
owned by the Canadian Pacific Railroad. All meditators
are we, here to study & practice the glorious Buddhadharma path
I learned I'm pregnant before I left home, need soda crackers
and plenty of calcium.

Everyone, including baby bones needs calcium
It's good when you've been "sitting" neck stiff as a glacier
And your thoughts are fractured soda crackers
The workmen are hammering & sawing loudly in the Chateau
When you have a free moment you rush to the snowy path
which stretches across Lake Louise to the frozen blue waterfall.
                                        Meditators

are walking too, some snap pictures, the skiers are not meditators
although they do a kind of meditation. Sunlight provides calcium
to everyone outside on a ski path
When you hear a rumble it could be the moving of a glacier
You can even hear this inside the Chateau
Walking with morning sickness you munch on soda crackers

The sound of the words "soda crackers"
brings me to attention. It's like when meditators
hear the shrine room gong. The Chateau
is bathed in light of white calcium
& maybe there's a tea break & some glacier
cake. There's always a sweet with tea, gives energy on the disciplined
                                        path

I wish I could go out with you to the narrow path
under the scented firs, there would be no need for soda crackers
to make me well. We could have tea at the Teahouse of the Six Glaciers
& live in caves like the ancient meditators
& get all the calcium
we want from the sun, & when we crave baths & postcards
visit the vast Chateau

Ah but it's warmer in the Chateau
when you are pregnant you can always take the path

to the kitchen for milk & oranges out of the refrigerator marked
          "prostrators & pregnant ladies" filled with hard boiled calcium
& maybe the special outing to Banff will bring soda crackers
you ordered, along with the other special dietary needs of meditators
who sit calmly, inscrutably, primally, like glaciers.

The glacier is kingly on the postcard, it dwarfs the Chateau
that this week houses World Cup skiers as well as meditators, paths crossing in
the lobby, do skiers need soda crackers?
They are certainly fortified by calcium.

Vajradhatu Seminary
Lake Louise
February 2, 1980

Complaints of a Seminarian

Have you ever been imprisoned in the middle of a glacier? This
    happened to a troop of boy scouts around here in the fifties

Actually I'm inside an old slightly run-down Canadian chateau
    & not supposed to get distracted

Large white curtains are drawn in the shrine hall

There's gristle in my *kanji! Kanji* is boiled down rice gruel often
    made with meat stock & is served at 7 a.m. every morning

Cooks blame gluey rice on cheap brand. I signal with Buddha
    spoon "no more" but the server doesn't see me. You have
    to eat every morsel without sauce

Hammering knock at door 6:30 am with bells nudges you
    rudely out of sexy dream

Other dreams are claustrophobic, as small as this room: I dream
    all the typewriter ribbons I've ever used are unwound &
    wrapped around my neck; I dream teacher comes to
    reprimand me in room & I cower like tiny mouse behind
    the radiator squeaking "But I'm pregnant, I'm pregnant! I
    need special privileges!"

Radiator humps & chirps all night even after you turn it off

My lips dry up

My face wrinkles like an old leaf

I'm nothing but a dusty Tibetan mummy

I sweat over monster pots & pans like scullery maid during dinner "clean-up." They are as big as truck wheels, oil drums & massive furnitures. My arms expand into the soapy trough

I'm in a galley I'm seasick all the time

I'm on a space station that's lost contact with its earth-ghetto

Mail is abominably slow. Customs people in Calgary want me to pay $34 duty tax on 1 grapefruit, a watch & my old black sleep shades from home — are they kidding?

I haven't seen a newspaper in months

I can't stop thinking of old lovers & dead people

I miss all my poetry books

Other people are really irritating: There's one guy who brings little candies in glassine wrappers into the shrine hall, opens them slowly, crinkles paper into ball and then has further audacity to suck on them loudly

It's really annoying when people have coughing fits for minutes on end, blow their noses incessantly & don't leave the shrine hall

Bathtub has no grate over the drain & big objects slip down there constantly. The maintenance man is immensely irritated although I give him a beer for his trouble (we're allowed to have "drinks" during study period). He had to haul in a dredging machine to dig up the brown washcloth & piece of sponge, and the heavy instrument scraped the white enamel tub

Food is alien & mysterious. Lunch today is pink rubber tubing

5 scallions glare up at me from *oryoki* bowl demanding to be eaten

The food chants are too fast, especially the "he" chant in the
   beginning: "He does not waste the roots of virtue. He is
   completely ornamented with all patience. He is the basis of
   the treasures of merit. He is adorned with the minor marks.
   He blossoms with the flowers of the major marks" etc. I
   like to say these words more slowly & think about them

The *umdze* starts the chants too low tonight as if we're all
   baritones

There's a draft in the meditation hall that sweeps at me right
   across the kidneys

The teacher makes Tsultim the monk open all the windows in
   the room before he lectures & everyone runs for blankets

The teacher is telling anecdotes about theism so fast I can't take
   notes

The *geko* is like a predator stalking the shrine room looking for
   victims whose posture he can correct. Vexing to have this
   odd fellow breathing down your neck & staring at your
   back: will he pounce?

My mind gradually unwinds—is that a complaint?

The last straw is lasagna made with tofu

There are 3 pay telephones as well as 3 pay washing machines for
   300 people

That stern woman gatekeeper gives me a scornful look because
        I'm nauseous all the time. One day she said to me, "Hold it,
        try to hold it!"

My legs fall asleep I shake them like a holy roller

My varicose veins throb & grow like blue mold

The text about the pain of being in the womb by Gampopa
        that was read today got me worried: "During the first week in
        the mother's womb a being is boiled and fried as in a warm
        vessel" and "In the seventh week there arises the so-called
        'clasping wind', and by its 'touch' the hands and feet are
        produced. At this stage a pain is felt which makes the
        embryo think it is pulled up by a strong wind and spread
        out with a stick by someone." Finally to top it off the baby
        comes out of the womb with pain "as if being drawn
        through a net of iron wires"

I can't do *tonglen*—sending & receiving—practice properly. I
        keep sending out the poisons instead of taking them in &
        cursing my enemies. I have to remember we aren't studying
        voodoo

I get mad at You Know Who, have a violent fit & fall off my
        cushion

The mountains are flat & boring like a postcard today

I have to learn to put others before myself

My travel iron doesn't work

My clothes are too hot & tight

It's after midnight & all the refrigerators are locked. There's one
     of Arisha's slogans posted at the kitchen entrance saying
     "Don't expect more."

Vajradhatu Seminary
Lake Louise
April 1980

Animals

My belly & breasts turn into a lumpy cow's

In a dream, Susan lifts out a translucent orange & shouts "It's a boy!"

Dr. Mary plays the heartbeat for me on a small black box

It sounds like ponies running in the wind

"That's the placenta wind," she says

Mike explains baby will go through all animal stages before birth

My heart is elephantine

I have a whale's appetite

Last night, creature fluttered inside me like a caught bird.

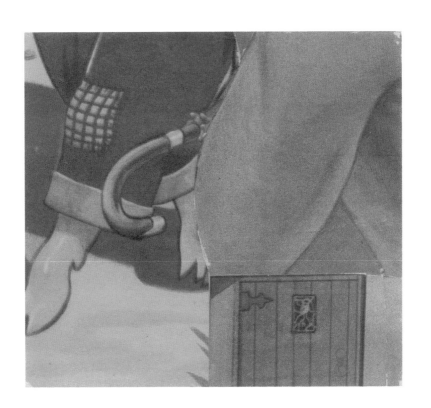

Enceinte

Mossy rock, tree limb, foot of a rabbit, large edible root, serpent lashing from side to side, a cushion, veiled lamp, some kind of moveable parts doll deity, sponge, rising loaf, butterfly, trapped bird, wax, mold, flame, a small man writing, small woman eating & lifting elbow, a bat, succulent plant, something in the oven, a potato doll, a doll of seashells, sandbag, large fish swimming in circles, a clock, something silent, a silent toy car, a memory, coiled & striking, fish hidden behind rock, every color & no color, a telephone receiver, a submarine, rubber expanding, held together with rubber bands, labial, fingers playing an instrument, inflatable doll, a school of dolphins, a tidal wave, unease, planet with circling rings, not made in a lab, a thunder storm, lashing out, a chest of toys, sedentary monkey, jack-in-a-box, icebox, lamps going on, a solar system, a tiny city ruled by a cobra, a city of clam inhabitants, an excursion, a place with hats on, an owl, a bear in a cave, drifting raft, boat on the waves, electricity, dancing flame's shadow on your face, bulging package, a rushed person gesturing excitedly as in hailing a speeding taxi cab, quicksilver.

8/9's

Languor, uselessness & general swamp I'd be or
        am proclivity to lie down, catch how
        certainly large I'm being, more food to
        hungry belly-dweller, conversant in
        lambent things, long talk, room for
        growing feet, infant cloth feet, animal
        feet or simply sing about the animals,
        naming their delicate

Suede buttresses: buttes, metamorphic rocks,
        gravidly mesozoic. Stages of all you
        could ever be: tadpole, butterfly
        (Colorado Marble or Alexandra's Sulphur),
        fish (Rainbow Trout, Squawfish, Northern
        Sucker), reptile (Western Skink), Spadefoot
        Toad, Rufous-sided Towhee I can't go on
        indefinitely listing but also include
        tender plants in a fertile

Soup. Also imagine the tree of vessels in
        placenta, the yolk sac, pale anemic
        vesicle under amnion, subcutis, corium,
        sebaceous glands, maxilla, at this stage:
        fish or frog or young bird. It
        flutters but never flies away. 8/9's of
        the way through it's a luminous,
        kicking, spiky, weighty, hiccoughing
        roving traveler.

Song: Time Drawes Neere

Time drawes neere
    love adornes you
        pours down autumn sunne

Babye I follow you
    sweete offspringe of
        nighte & sleepe

Pangs of the babye
    tossed in a bellie:
        birdies & woodlands cheer!

Eies gaze with delighte
    I hope I fear I laugh
        call you "rolling mountain"

Your roote is deepe, be you englishe
    rosie fayre or german darkly
        call you boy or girl?

I must have pillows & musicke
    I must have raspberry leaf tea
        I needs must groan Ah me!

Ah thee! A secret growing
    I go no more a-maying
        I settle into my tent shift

Bursting at seams
    big tub, water barrel
        tossed as boat or cloud, gravid

Powre to claime my hart in
    bodye roome, powre to keepe
        me waking all nighte a-peeing

I ride you unseene wave
    wee rise together
        under daddye's roof & hand.

Number Song

I've multiplied, I'm 2.
He was part of me,
he came out of me,
he took a part of me.
He took me apart.
I'm 2, he's my art,
no, he's separate.
He art one. I'm not
done & I'm still one.
I sing of my son. I've
multiplied. My heart's
in 2, half to him &
half to you,
who are also a part
of him, & you & he
& I make trio of
kind congruity.

Scallop Song

I wore a garland of the briar that put me now in awe

I wore a garland of the brain that was whole

It commanded me, done babbling

And I no more blabbed, spare no lie

Tell womanhood she shake off pity

Tell the man to give up tumult for the while

To wonder at the sight of baby's beauty

Ne let the monsters fray us with things that not be

From a high tower poem issuing

Everything run along in creation til I end the song

Ne none fit for so wild beasts

Ne none so joyous, ne none no give no lie

Tell old woes to leave off here:

I sing this into a scallop shell with face of a pearl

& leave all sorrow bye & bye.

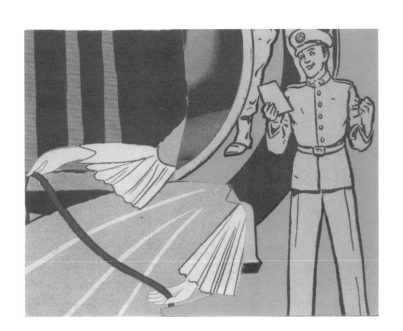

Rondeau

Is there any Heaven
Any Heaven but loving?

No, no heaven but loving

Is there any Heaven at all

She who holds yielding baby
in arms is in Heaven

Is there any Heaven
Any Heaven but loving?

You see me loving him
This is heaven

To Baby

"A little Saint best fits a little shrine"

What you are makes me grow
  younger to meet you.
    Everything gets new,
     lacks death. Heart
      sighs "Beauty"
       rocking lamb
        to sleep.

While you cry, wind pauses
  to learn the sound, then
   applauds a loud lung.
    You wear a dreamy
     nightgown painted
      clouds float
       upon.

We all agree babies are
  amazement. See, world,
   how guileless & mild
    is he. Smell every-
     where Ivory Snow.
      Hear him suck
       tenderly.

What makes the cabin fresh?
  Infant flesh! Huddled
   against a tiny body,
    a body doting
     sings to you:

Rest your head my darling
Wee baby one
The stars are out
The canyon sleeps
Your life has just begun.

Assent

Disastrous world—does it see me watching?

Hard world—how can it work?

My mind would break
over someone's hatred

Disastrous world—out of control

I can't bow down but to baby.

December Song

Here is a song I sought to sing you
  migrant thoughts I sought to capture
    & sought all manner of words to rhyme
     in a sparkle, the deficient sentimental
     tongue cries I am emotional! yes,
      that you would hear me crying &
      guess the reason, unlock your
       stubborn reason & seek a
       calmer season. I sought
       to heal the lesion &
        only way to sing is as
        new mother gibbering

The baby calls! & that is luscious feeling
  The baby moves! & that is luscious seeing
  We tumble the house we shake the rug
  We rock the cradle we dump the tub
  Don't throw the baby out with the
    bathwater we say. We cheer & weep
    & all the memories we keep locked
    in a book, the book of Baby's
      Eyes, & we think we grow wise
      & baby grows wise

Winter smiles on us, nights are gentle
  wind rings the holy porch bell
    & when we want intrusion
     we listen to the radio report the worldly inferno!
     Iran wants 9 billion dollar guarantee
      or else more people are still in captivity
      how things are stalled, everyone's
      appalled, are lives or honor
       more important over all—
       has the president failed?
        Rebellious inmates launch
         explosive operation in Turino

Seismologists speak of another eruption, more
volcano disaster relief, more ABSCAM
corruption. O to stimulate the eyes of the
beholder. A hero a poet a singer gets shot
then we get older.

O bonnie lad, dear bonnie growing boy: Natives
declare a 2,900 square mile zone for fishing
rights solution and speaking of evolution, the creationists
are trying a new tactic, one that isn't so static
stripping religion from the creation account
& supplying speakers in schools to argue
that supernatural processes were required
for the origin of our universe, inspired
amino acids could not have taken
place by chance, what is this
marvelous human dance?

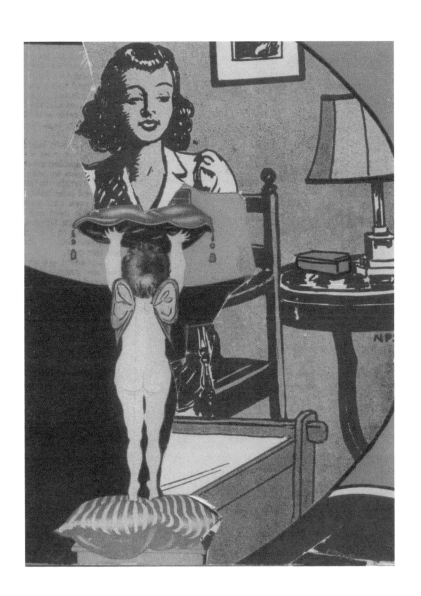

Complaynt

after Emily Dickinson

I'm wanton—no I've stopped that,
That old place
I've changed, I'm Mother
It's more mysterious.
How odd the past looks
When I reread old notebooks,
See their faces fade
I feel it everywhere
& ordinary too
Am I safer now?
Was other way gayer?
I'm Mother now, O help &
Continue!

In the Downfill USA Store

"This is the littlest one I ever held!"
says ruddy teen salesgirl, excited
amidst racks of bright puffy vests
as I hand the baby over
to try purple one on.

Baby's Pantoum

for Reed

I lie in my crib midday this is
        unusual I don't sleep really
Mamma's sweeping or else boiling water for tea
        Other sounds are creak of chair & floor, water
        dripping on heater from laundry, cat licking itself

Unusual I don't sleep really
        unless it's dark night everyone in bed
Other sounds are creak of chair & floor, water
dripping on heater from laundry, cat licking itself
        & occasional peck on typewriter, peck on my cheek

Unless it's dark night everyone in bed
        I'm wide awake hungry wet lonely thinking
occasional peck on typewriter, peck on my cheek
        My brain cells grow, I get bigger

I'm wide awake wet lonely hungry thinking
        Then Mamma pulls out breast, says "milky?"
My brain cells grow, I get bigger
        This is my first Christmas in the world

Mamma pulls out breast, says "milky?"
        Daddy conducts a walking tour of house
This is my first Christmas in the world
        I study knots in pine wood ceiling

Daddy conducts a walking tour of house
        I study pictures of The Madonna del Parto, a
        sweet-faced Buddha & Papago Indian girl
I study knots in pine wood ceiling
        I like contrasts, stripes, eyes & hairlines

I study pictures of The Madonna del Parto, a
sweet-faced Buddha & Papago Indian girl
        Life is colors, faces are moving
I like contrasts, stripes, eyes & hairlines
        I don't know what I look like

Life is colors, faces are moving
        They love me smiling
I don't know what I look like
        I try to speak of baby joys & pains

They love me smiling
        She takes me through a door, the wind howls
I try to speak of baby joys & pains
        I'm squinting, light cuts through my skin

She takes me through a door, the wind howls
        Furry shapes & large vehicles move close
I'm squinting, light cuts through my skin
        World is vast I'm in it with closed eyes

Furry shapes & large vehicles move close
        I rest between her breasts, she places me on dry leaves
World is vast I'm in it with closed eyes
        I'm locked in little dream, my fists are tight

I rest between her breasts, she places me on dry leaves
        He carries me gently on his chest & shoulder
I'm locked in little dream, my fists are tight
        They showed me moon in sky, was something
        in my dream

He carries me gently on his chest & shoulder
        He calls me sweet baby, good baby boy
They showed me moon in sky, was something
in my dream
        She is moving quickly & dropping things

He calls me sweet baby, good baby boy
        She sings hush go to sleep right now
She is moving quickly & dropping things
        They rock my cradle, they hold me tightly in their arms

She sings hush go to sleep right now
        She wears red nightgown, smells of spice & milk
They rock my cradle, they hold me tightly in their arms
        I don't know any of these words or things yet

She wears a red nightgown, smells of spice & milk
        He has something woolen and rough on
I don't know any of these words or things yet
        I sit in my chair & watch what moves

He has something woolen & rough on
        I can stretch & unfold as he holds me in the bath
I sit in my chair & watch what moves
        I see when things are static or they dance

I can stretch & unfold as he holds me in the bath
        Water is soft I came from water
I can see when things are static or they dance
        like flames, the cat pouncing, shadows or light
        streaming in

Water is soft I came from water
        Not that long ago I was inside her
like flames, the cat pouncing, shadows or light
streaming in
        I heard her voice then I remember now

Not that long ago I was inside her
        I lie in my crib midday this is
always changing, I am expanding toward you
        Mamma's sweeping or else boiling water for tea.

Sonne

Could
anything
mean more to me
right now
than the
boy's smile
as he turns
on belly
lifting his face—

his
muscles
get
stronger

he laughs
throwing his
head back
as I toss him
around my lap

and he wants
to put the purple iris
inside
his pink mouth

no no
no no no, nothing.

King

the king sits
in his courtyard
on brocade
pillows,
rattle-sceptre
in hand

little doll:
don't grow up
be our ruler
forever
in this
lilac garden

"buzz saw"

buzz saw
bird caw
fly *zzzzz*
wake him
shoo!

baby
imitates
splash
in the
lake

sneezes
"choo"
Bless you!

Museum Madonnas in Massachusetts

Ouch! Hairy red angels flank Taddeo di Bartolo's
Madonna of Humility, and the babe's finger's
stuck in a bird's beak,

while little Jesus yanks on the shawl of Aretino's Madonna.

What's this luscious baby doing with those strawberries?

The Master of the Female Half-Lengths got off on this one.

I love the angel with parrot wings

but how much more lovely is the Madonna
by the Master of the Embroidered Foliage.

Someone tilted this baby's feet up
to make them shapely

and now he's cramped and cranky.

Napping in the Shadow of Day

The house is still that shook with glee
Where did it go?
The shades pulled down
No one to phone
Silence the music, the clock
Baby is sleeping like a locket
His body ran down
Hush when you visit
Don't knock nor fidget
The day sits waiting
You must too
Hush he's lightly breathing

Nursing Ambrose on the "A" Train

2 young black women—sisters?
& 2 children—a boy, maybe 6
girl a bit older
sit directly across from us
look directly my way nonplussed
then turn shyly

A glare from maybe she's Greek
a little down the car to my left
(I stare her down)

An enormous black middleaged Church lady
— 300 pounds? — gets on
& Larry says
"I'd like that woman to take care of me"
Suddenly there's another giantess
bigger than the first
sitting next to her
"I'd like both of those women
to take care of me"

I say we're already inside them,
bobbing & sleeping.

Baby & the Gypsy

Wizened elf woman
crouched over sink
in Ladies' Room
at O'Hare Airport
looks up, sees us
in mirror, her eyes wide

    — Oh a baby!
     Let me hold the baby
     You take your time, dearie

She holds him like an icon
while I wash my face

    — He's got a future, this one
     He'll break some hearts
     Don't you worry about that!

Science Show

Baby's keen eye
is fixed
on epoxy tube
to squeeze it
claim it
know it

We watch a
TV show
in which
iguanas emerge
from sea
to bask
in sun

It starts
them up

& solar heating
is indicated
in the spiky
plates of
a dinosaur

Crocodiles care
assiduously
for their
eggs
& once hatched,
a young one
sits in
mother's
big maw
like a
cockpit

To Lure to Him the Objects
of the World He So Desires

white typewriter alphabet keys come to baby
Vajrasattva don't topple down on top of baby
Skrip Ink don't spill on baby
press button, room light up for baby
Chinese dragon of moving red mouth, green shirt on, come
        grasp the baby's finger
electric clock buzz for baby
telephone ring for baby
Yellow Pages fall onto baby's lap
little cork to baby's mouth
Bozo-On-A-Holiday approach baby on your ratchety wheels
Mickey Mouse, baby holds you
measuring spoons, baby shakes you
Hildegard the Duck with undulating neck come to baby's arms
shiny green traveling trunk you hold baby's woolens
baby loves to encounter a toothbrush
baby would love a red caboose
Phoebe Unicorn you are a pretty toy, come to baby
Baby sees tapestry unicorn in the museum
Lady's Lucky Locker with tiny implements inside, come to
      baby's hands

All the Stoned Wheat Thins make their way to baby
pink highheels you make hammers for baby
baby loves the protuberances of any object
spotted shells of the South Pacific come to baby
arroyos run to baby
bowling pins you get knocked over
tupperware come to baby
Mozart Concerti sing in baby's ears
he loves a shiny black disc
Mr. Saheeb the Camel do a baby's jig
Aquaman, swim to baby
green-eyed owl hoot for baby
gruff bear sings the Brahms lullaby for baby
workboots are clumsy in baby's lap with their laces dangling
wooden block necklace, baby wears you like a lei
books-a-plenty, don't let baby rip your pages out
satin half-moon cradle baby's neck
Hindu horse take baby for a magical ride
prehistoric cave animal with shadows on your pelt, you
          are baby's favorite
flute makes a toot
socks leap to baby's kicking feet

Little Lover

after Paul Eluard

He stands on my eyelids
light as toast
His silky hair's blocked
my face
His hands talk like mine
but his eyes are grey
Grey like a stone!
He's swallowed up
by my tall shadow
like stars in daylight
He has his eyes open
and never lets me sleep
(I miss sleep)
O little boy
your dreams make
cares evaporate
but I'm still exhausted
You wake saying "My noodle,
My noodle!"
Your dreams make me laugh
Weep & laugh
& speak with everything to say.

Baby's Second Pantoum

a year after the first

I walk toward Daddy
     to grab his legs & laugh
He is my friend I watch him closely
     I clap & spin, the telephone rings

To grab his legs & laugh
     I do this repeatedly & tumble on the floor
I clap & spin, the telephone rings
     I pick it up & put it in their bed

I do this repeatedly & tumble on the floor
     A motorcar chases me across the floor
I pick it up & put it in their bed
     Someone squawking at the other end

A motorcar chases me across the floor
     It clacks & whirrs along the rug
Someone squawking at the other end
     I put one thing inside another

It clacks & whirrs along the rug
     I place a lid on top of a container
I put one thing inside another
     like spools in cups, raisins in a sieve

I place a lid on top of a container
     Dogs barking outside the window
like spools in cups, raisins in a sieve
     I go after a cat named "Chase"

Dogs barking outside my window
     I hug my blanket when I awake
I go after a cat named "Chase"
     Who is soft & fits inside my neck

I hug my blanket when I awake
     A musical pillow sits on my head
It is soft & fits inside my neck
     I stand on the highchair to be tall

A musical pillow sits on top of my head
     I wear a bib that catches many crumbs
I stand on the highchair to be tall
     They laugh with me & lift me to their faces

I wear a bib that catches many crumbs
     I don't like soap in my eyes
They laugh with me & lift me to their faces
     I sing "hot tea" when the kettle whistles

I don't like soap in my eyes
　　　but love to splash & watch the water run
And sing "hot tea" when the kettle whistles
　　　I enjoy standing in the refrigerator door

But love to splash & watch the water run
　　　& see pigeons between high buildings
I enjoy standing in the refrigerator door
　　　& screw up my nose at babyface in mirror

& see pigeons between high buildings
　　　I get very still in my stroller
& screw up my nose at babyface in mirror
　　　She reads a book about a bunny in a green room

I get very still in my stroller
　　　The bunny says goodnight to everything in his world
She reads a book about a bunny in a green room
　　　I know some voices, names & faces too

The bunny says goodnight to everything in his world
　　　I turn away from the picture of the old woman
I know some voices names & faces too
　　　A nightmare makes me start up in my crib

I turn away from the picture of the old woman
    I jump up & pull the books down from their shelves
A nightmare makes me start up in my crib
    My teeth hurt & need to bite

I jump up & pull the books down from their shelves
    Then roll a ball under Mamma's desk
My teeth hurt & need to bite
    I shout "No!" & wildly shake my head

Then roll a ball under Mamma's desk
    Shirts come swiftly over my head
I shout "No!" & wildly shake my head
    I grab their noses & laugh

Shirts come swiftly over my head
    I beat on pots & pans & rip envelopes apart
I grab their noses & laugh
    & point to light

I beat on pots & pans & rip envelopes apart
    I walk toward Daddy
& point to light
    He is my friend I watch him closely.

Mother & Child

Child: What is the destination of the sunlight's particles?

Mother: Your hair, of course. Atoms of light created for your beauty, your beauty's articles

Child: And where do roses go when they fade?

Mother: Into your beauty, where they sleep in the shade

Child: And where does the nightingale fly when she stops singing?

Mother: Into your mouth where she continues singing until the seasons come round again

Child: And what about the falling stars, where do they go?

Mother: Into your eyes where they twinkle, as if you didn't know

Child: And where goes the Phoenix, that magical bird which alternately burns and rises from its own ashes?

Mother: It builds its nest of immortality upon your little breast, my child, under your innocent lashes

Poem

for her who bore me
               & by whose sorrows
        I am cast down:
she more dauntless than I'll ever be
        I loved her tenacity
            &
        accepte her prerogative
       to complayne of incapacity
O mystique language of mother's heart
        to her childe
       It's here in the room
        searing me now.

Anne Waldman has been an active member of the "Outrider" experimental poetry community for over 40 years as writer, sprechstimme performer, professor, editor, "magpie" scholar, infra-structure and cultural/political activist. She grew up on Macdougal Street in Greenwich Village where she still lives part-time, and bi-furcated to Boulder, Colorado in 1974 when she co-founded The Jack Kerouac School of Disembodied Poetics with Allen Ginsberg at Naropa University, the first Buddhist inspired school in the West. She currently serves as Artistic Director of its celebrated Summer Writing program. Allen Ginsberg has called her his "spiritual wife." She is the author of over 40 books of poetry including *Kill or Cure, Marriage: A Sentence, Structure of the World Compared to a Bubble, Red Noir*, and the poetic text: *Outrider*. Her most recent book-length poem is *Manatee/Humanity* (Penguin Poets 2009). She is also the author of the legendary *Fast Speaking Woman* (City Lights, San Francisco), now translated into Italian, Czech and French, as well as the 800 page epic *Iovis* trilogy (Coffee House Press). She is editor of *The Beat Book* (Shambhala Publications) and co-editor of *The Angel Hair Anthology* (Granary Books), *Civil Disobediences: Poetics and Politics in Action* (Coffee House) and *Beats at Naropa* (Coffee House 2009). A book of her poems translated into Chinese is forthcoming in 2009.

She has worked extensively with her son, musician and composer Ambrose Bye, for whom and "out of" whom *First Baby Poems* was written 27 years ago. Their collaborations include the CDs *In the Room of Never Grieve, Eye of the Falcon* and *Matching Half*, also with Akilah Oliver. Ambrose has been a constant muse and inspiration for her own work.

George Schneeman has shown his work — paintings, collages, pottery, calendars and frescoes — at the Minneapolis Museum of Fine Arts, the Denver Art Museum, and in New York at the Fischbach Gallery, the Holly Solomon Galley, the Donohue/Sosinski Gallery and the CUE Art Foundation, among others. Three of his collaborative books have been published by Granary Books: *Homage to Allen G.* (with Anne Waldman), *In Nam What Can Happen?* (with Ted Berrigan), and *Yodeling into a Kotex* (with Ron Padgett). He has worked extensively with poets for decades. Schneeman makes his home in New York and spends part of each year in Tuscany. Granary also published *The Collaborative Art of George Schneeman*, edited by Ron Padgett in 2004.

Made in the USA